RAMADAN

HASSAB BIN AHMED

Ramadan

First edition - 2023-02-25

Published by notionpress, India

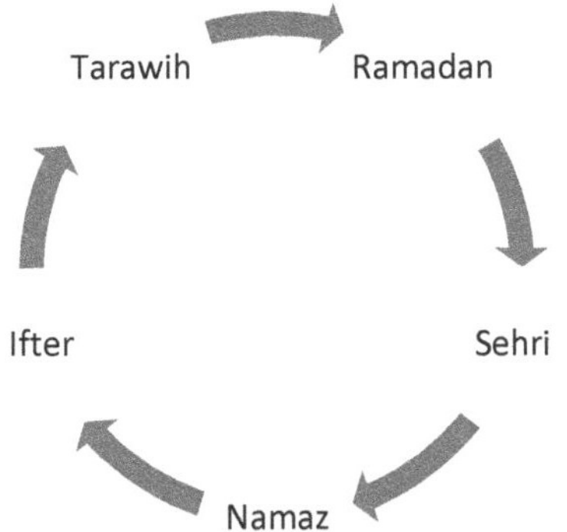

O you who have believed, decreed upon you is fasting as it was decreed upon those before you that you may become righteous

-

Al-Baqara: Ayah No. 183

PREFACE TO THE FIRST EDITION

Ramadan is one of the most sacred and significant months in the Islamic calendar. It is a time of spiritual reflection, prayer, and fasting for Muslims all around the world. This month holds great importance in the hearts of Muslims, as it is believed to be the month in which the Holy Quran was revealed to Prophet Muhammad (peace be upon him).

I have not studied any Islamic subject. So in this book, I did not give any kind of fatwa and did not try to give it. Because I think I don't even have the minimum qualification to give a fatwa. I've always tried to make references to this book. It can still go wrong. Because to err is human. So if you see any mistake, you must forgive as a younger brother. With this hope, I started the journey of Ramadan

Hassab bin ahmed

25-02-2023

ABOUT THE AUTHOR

Hassab bin Ahmed was born in 1999 in Assam, India. Although he followed religion with his father when he was young, at one point he went far away from religion. In 2017, by the grace of Allah, he returned to religion and is trying to spread Islam. Hassab bin graduated from Guwahati University in 2021.

Ramadan: Month of Fasting

Ramadan is one of the most sacred and significant months in the Islamic calendar. It is a time of spiritual reflection, prayer, and fasting for Muslims all around the world. This month holds great importance in the hearts of Muslims, as it is believed to be the month in which the Holy Quran was revealed to Prophet Muhammad (peace be upon him).

Fasting during Ramadan is one of the five pillars of Islam, which are the fundamental practices that every Muslim is obligated to follow. During this month, Muslims fast from dawn until sunset, abstaining from food, drink, and other physical needs. The act of fasting is not only a means of fulfilling one's religious duty, but it is also a way to purify the soul, increase self-discipline, and develop empathy for those who are less fortunate.

Ramadan is also a time for increased acts of worship, including prayer and recitation of the Quran. Muslims strive to improve their spiritual connection with Allah (God) through these acts of devotion. They also focus on practicing good deeds such as giving charity, helping others, and showing kindness and compassion towards their fellow human beings.

In addition to the spiritual benefits, Ramadan is also a time for families and communities to come together. Muslims break their fast at sunset with a meal called iftar, which is often shared with family and friends. Many mosques and Islamic centers also provide iftar meals for those who may not have the means to prepare their own.

The month of Ramadan concludes with the celebration of Eid al-Fitr, which is a joyous festival that marks the end of fasting. Muslims gather for prayer and celebrations, exchanging gifts and sharing meals with loved ones.

Overall, Ramadan is a month of self-reflection, spiritual growth, and communal solidarity. It is a time to detach from worldly desires and connect with the divine. Through fasting, prayer, and acts of kindness, Muslims strive to become better versions of themselves and strengthen their relationship with Allah.

.....

Benefits of the Ramadan Fast According to Modern Science

❖ Reduces Hypertension

A new study published in The American Journal of Medicine shows that short-term intermittent fasting can help reduce hypertension or high blood pressure. This study contributes to a growing body of research showing that intermittent fasting can help improve heart health and reduce the risk for hypertension and other cardiovascular diseases.

❖ Increases Brain Function

Fasting has also been shown to have numerous brain benefits, such as higher levels of nerve growth factor (NGF). This protein helps regulate neurons' growth, maintenance, proliferation, and survival. NGF is essential for neurons' growth and normal function in both the peripheral and central nervous systems. Fasting also increases the expression of brain-derived neurotrophic factor (BDNF), a protein that supports the survival of existing brain cells and encourages the growth of new ones. Low levels of BDNF have been attributed to an increased risk for Alzheimer's disease.

❖ Improves Body Composition

Fasting has been known to improve body composition. This means it can reduce the percentage of body fat a person has while increasing their muscle mass and overall health.

❖ Fasting Reduces Cancer Risk

It's true! Fasting can help you reduce your risk of cancer. But how? Cancer cells cannot process ketones produced by the liver from fat and fatty acids when in a fasted state. Simply put, fasting helps starve cancer cells and makes them more susceptible to the body's immune system.

❖ Stimulates Autophagy

Fasting stimulates autophagy, which is the process by which cells and tissues recycle damaged components. It's what allows your cells to renew themselves and survive without starving. Autophagy promotes longevity and helps prevent conditions associated with aging, including cancer, heart disease, and neurodegenerative disorders such as Parkinson's disease and Alzheimer's disease.

❖ Lowers Inflammation

Fasting lowers inflammation, which is a significant cause of aging. This is because fasting triggers changes in your gut microbiota. After fasting, the gut microbiome becomes richer in bacteria with anti-inflammatory properties.

❖ Regulates Sleep Patterns

Fasting has long been associated with healthy sleep. The first thing to know is that fasting does have an impact on your sleep—it can help regulate your circadian rhythm (your natural sleep cycle) and make it easier to fall asleep at night.

❖ Normalizes Ghrelin Levels

Fasting normalizes ghrelin levels, a hormone responsible for hunger and the body's response to fasting. This is important because fasting helps you lose weight without feeling excessively hungry, unlike many other diets.

.....

Importance of Ramadan

Ramadan is considered the most important month in the Islamic calendar, as it holds great spiritual significance for Muslims worldwide. This holy month marks the time when Allah revealed the first verses of the Quran to the Prophet Muhammad, and it is a time of heightened devotion, prayer, and reflection for Muslims around the world. Here are some of the key reasons why Ramadan is so important in Islam:

1.REVELATION OF THE QURAN:

Muslims believe that the Quran was first revealed to Prophet Muhammad (peace be upon him) during the month of Ramadan. This event is known as "Laylat al-Qadr" (the Night of Power), which is considered to be one of the holiest nights of the year.

2.FASTING:

Fasting during Ramadan is one of the Five Pillars of Islam, which are the fundamental practices of the faith. Muslims abstain from food, drink, and other physical needs from dawn until sunset, as a way of purifying their souls and focusing on their spiritual growth. Fasting is seen as a way of developing self-discipline and empathy for those who are less fortunate, and it serves as a reminder of the importance of living a humble and compassionate life.

3.QURAN:

Ramadan is a time for Muslims to read and reflect on the Quran, which is considered the holy book of Islam. It is believed that the Quran was revealed to the Prophet Muhammad during the month of Ramadan, and so reading and studying the Quran during this time holds particular significance. Many Muslims aim to read the entire Quran during the month of Ramadan, as a way of deepening their understanding of their faith and strengthening their connection to Allah.

4.COMMUNITY:

Ramadan is a time of increased community and family gatherings, as Muslims come together to break their fasts each evening. This communal breaking of the fast, called iftar, is a time of joy and celebration, and it serves as a reminder of the importance of unity and compassion in Islam. Muslims also gather in mosques for special prayers and sermons, further strengthening the bonds of community and fostering a sense of belonging.

5.CHARITY:

Giving to those in need is an important part of Islam, and this is especially emphasized during Ramadan. Muslims are encouraged to be generous and charitable during this holy month, donating money and resources to those who are less fortunate. This serves as a reminder of the importance of helping others and living a life of service and compassion.

In conclusion, Ramadan is a time of great importance and significance in Islam. Through fasting, prayer, reflection, and community, Muslims strive to deepen their connection to Allah and to each other, while also practicing important values such as self-discipline, empathy, and generosity. Ramadan serves as a reminder of the importance of living a humble and compassionate life, and it inspires Muslims to strive for spiritual growth and to embody the values of Islam in their daily lives.

...

productive Ramadan

Ramadan is a month of spirituality, reflection, and self-improvement. It is also a time to focus on productivity and making the most of our time. Here are some tips for a productive Ramadan:

❖ SET GOALS:

Start by setting specific goals for what you want to accomplish during the month of Ramadan. It can be anything from reading a certain number of pages from the Quran each day, to finishing a book, to exercising regularly. Having clear goals will help you stay focused and motivated.

❖ MANAGE YOUR TIME:

With the changes in your daily routine during Ramadan, it is important to manage your time wisely. Prioritize your tasks and allocate your time accordingly. Make sure to schedule time for prayer, Quran recitation, and other religious activities.

❖ EAT HEALTHILY:

Eating healthy and balanced meals during Ramadan is essential for maintaining energy levels and staying productive. Avoid overeating or eating heavy meals that can make you feel sluggish. Instead, focus on eating foods that provide sustained energy, such as complex carbohydrates, lean proteins, and fruits and vegetables.

❖ STAY HYDRATED:

While fasting, it is important to stay hydrated by drinking enough water during non-fasting hours. Dehydration can lead to fatigue and decreased productivity. Drinking water regularly can help keep you alert and focused.

❖ MINIMIZE DISTRACTIONS:

Minimize distractions during the day by turning off notifications on your phone or limiting your use of social media. This will help you stay focused on your goals and make the most of your time.

❖ ENGAGE IN ACTS OF KINDNESS:

Engaging in acts of kindness, such as volunteering, donating to charity, or helping others, can help you feel fulfilled and productive during Ramadan. These activities not only benefit others but also help you develop a sense of purpose and meaning.

❖ REFLECT AND SELF-IMPROVE:

Ramadan is a time for self-reflection and self-improvement. Take time to reflect on your habits, behaviors, and attitudes, and work on improving yourself. Identify areas where you can improve, set goals, and take action to make positive changes in your life.

In conclusion, Ramadan can be a highly productive month if you approach it with intention and focus. By setting goals, managing your time, eating healthily, staying hydrated, minimizing distractions, engaging in acts of kindness, and reflecting on your self-improvement, you can make the most of this month and achieve your personal and spiritual goals.

. . .

Preparation before fasting

If you are planning to fast, there are several things you can do to prepare your body and mind for the experience. some tips:

❖ **CONSULT YOUR DOCTOR:**
If you have any medical conditions or are taking any medications, it's important to talk to your doctor before starting a fast.

❖ **STAY HYDRATED:**
 Drink plenty of water before and during your fast to help prevent dehydration.

❖ **EAT A BALANCED DIET:**
Eat a healthy, balanced diet leading up to your fast to ensure your body has the nutrients it needs.

❖ **AVOID CAFFEINE:**
 Caffeine can dehydrate you and make it more difficult to fast.

❖ **PLAN YOUR MEALS:**
If you are doing a multi-day fast, plan your meals carefully for the days leading up to and following the fast to help ease your body in and out of the fasting state.

❖ **MANAGE STRESS:**

Try to minimize stress as much as possible leading up to your fast. Stress can cause your body to release cortisol, which can make it more difficult to fast.

❖ **REST:**

Make sure you get plenty of rest leading up to your fast, as your body will need extra energy during the fasting period.

❖ **BE MINDFUL:**

Take time to mentally prepare for your fast, and practice mindfulness and relaxation techniques to help you stay focused and centered during the fast.

.....

Ramadan on Monday and Thursday

I hope everyone is well, many of us want to keep nafal fast and many times we keep nafal fast. If we can fast on the day that Hazrat Muhammad (sw) used to fast then it is better if we fast. We know from Sahih Hadith that Hazrat Muhammad (sw) used to fast on Monday and Thursday. So we will try to fast these two days inshAllah.

❖ Aishah narrated:
"The Prophet used to try to fast on Mondays and Thursdays."(Sunan at-Tirmidhi (Islamic foundation)-743)

❖ Abu Hurairah narrated that:
the Messenger of Allah said: "Deeds are presented on Monday and Thursday, and I love that my deeds be presented while I am fasting."(Sunan at-Tirmidhi (Islamic foundation)-745)

❖ It was narrate from Jubair bin Nufair that 'Aishah said:
"The Messenger of Allah used to be keen to fast on Mondays and Thursday."(Sunan An-Nasai (Islamic foundation)-2362)

❖ It was narrated that 'Aishah said:

20

"The Messenger of Allah used to be keen to fast on Mondays and Thursday."(Sunan An-Nasai (Islamic foundation)-2363)

❖ Chapter: The Desirability of Observing Saum (Fasting) on Monday and Thursday

Abu Qatadah (May Allah be pleased with him) reported:
The Messenger of Allah (ﷺ) was asked about fasting on Mondays. He said, "That is the day on which I was born and the day on which I received Revelation."

[Muslim].

Commentary: This Hadith points out the excellence of fasting on Mondays. The reason behind this, as is stated in the Hadith, is that the Prophet (PBUH) was born on it and that it was the day on which he received the first Revelation(Riyad as-Salihin-1263)

❖ Narrated Usamah ibn Zayd:

The client of Usamah ibn Zayd said that he went along with Usamah to Wadi al-Qura in pursuit of his camels. He would fast on Monday and Thursday. His client said to him: Why do you fast on Monday and Thursday, while you are an old man? He said: The Prophet of Allah (ﷺ) used to fast on Monday and Thursday. When he was asked about it, he said: The works of the servants (of Allah) are presented (to

Allah) on Monday and Thursday.(Sunan Abu Dawood -2428)

❖ Abu Qatada al-Ansari (Allah be pleased with him) reported that the Messenger of Allah (ﷺ) was asked about his fasting. The Messenger of Allah (ﷺ) felt annoyed. Thereupon 'Umar (Allah be pleased with him) said:

We are pleased with Allah as the Lord, with Islam as our Code of Life, with Muhammad as the Messenger and with our pledge (to you for willing and cheerful submission) as a (sacred) commitment. He was then asked about perpetual fasting, whereupon he said: He neither fasted nor did he break it, or he did not fast and he did not break it. He was then asked about fasting for two days and breaking one day. He (the Holy Prophet) said: And who has strength enough to do it? He was asked about fasting for a day and breaking for two days, whereupon he said: May Allah bestow upon us strength to do it. He was then asked about fasting for a day and breaking on the other, whereupon he said: That is the fasting of my brother David (peace be upon him). He was then asked about fasting on Monday, whereupon he said: It was the day on which I was born. on which I was commissioned with prophethood or revelation was sent to me, (and he further) said: Three days' fasting every month and of the whole of Ramadan every year is a perpetual fast. He was asked about fasting on the day of 'Arafa (9th of Dhu'I-Hijja), whereupon he said: It expiates the sins of the preceding year and the coming year.

He was asked about fasting on the day of 'Ashura (10th of Muharram), whereupon be said: It expiates the sins of the preceding year. (Imam Muslim said that in this hadith there is a) narration of Imam Shu'ba that he was asked about fasting on Monday and Thursday, but we (Imam Muslim) did not mention Thursday for we found it as an error (in reporting).(Sahih Muslim (Hadith Academy)- 2637)

❖ Narrated Usamah ibn Zayd:

The client of Usamah ibn Zayd said that he went along with Usamah to Wadi al-Qura in pursuit of his camels. He would fast on Monday and Thursday. His client said to him: Why do you fast on Monday and Thursday, while you are an old man? He said: The Prophet of Allah (ﷺ) used to fast on Monday and Thursday. When he was asked about it, he said: The works of the servants (of Allah) are presented (to Allah) on Monday and Thursday.(Sunan Abu Dawood-2436)

❖ Narrated One of the wives of the Prophet:

Hunaydah ibn Khalid narrated from his wife on the authority of one of the wives of the Prophet (ﷺ) who said: The Messenger of Allah (ﷺ) used to fast the first nine days of Dhul-Hijjah, Ashura' and three days of every month, that is, the first Monday (of the month) and Thursday. (Sunan Abu Dawood-2437)

❖ Hunaidah Al-Khuza'i said:

"I entered upon the Mother of the Believers and heard her say: 'The Messenger of Allah used to fast three days of each month: The first Monday of the month, then Thursday, then the following Thursday."(Sunan An-Nasai (Islamic foundation)-2417)

.....

The Three Gifts Of Ramadan

The month of fasting is the month of mercy. The Holy Quran was revealed in this month. Today we will see only three gifts from the gifts that Almighty Allah has given in this month.

* It is mentioned in Sahih Bukhari Hadith No-38 that "Whoever fasts in Ramadan with faith and hoping for a reward from Allah, his sins will be forgiven."

* If for some reason your fast goes wrong and you are not forgiven, there is nothing to despair. Allah has given you another gift. It is mentioned in Sahih Bukhari Hadith No. 37 that it is said, "Whoever performs qiyaam (night prayer) in Ramadan with faith in the hope of reward from Allah, then his sins are forgiven."

* Suppose your fasting and qiyaam(night prayer) are both wrong. He has nothing to be disappointed about. Allah loves you and gave you another gift. It is mentioned in Sahih Bukhari Hadith No. 2014 that it is said "Whoever prays Lailatul Qadr with faith in the hope of reward from Allah, then his sins are forgiven."

All of us will perform these three acts of worship, inshallah. And if a person does not receive forgiveness despite having such a beautiful gift in this month, then there is no more suffering than him.

.....

IFTAR

Iftar is a significant religious observance for Muslims during the holy month of Ramadan. It marks the breaking of the day-long fast that is observed from dawn to sunset. The fast is considered as one of the five pillars of Islam, which also include the declaration of faith, prayer, charity, and pilgrimage to Mecca.

The word 'iftar' is derived from the Arabic word 'Futoor,' which means 'to break the fast.' Muslims around the world break their fast at the time of sunset, which is signaled by the call to prayer. The fast is broken with dates and water, followed by a hearty meal known as iftar.

Iftar is not just a meal but a time of celebration, socialization, and spiritual reflection. It is a time when Muslims gather with family and friends to share their blessings and break bread together. It is also a time to be grateful for the blessings that have been bestowed upon them and to seek forgiveness from Allah for their sins.

The iftar meal varies from country to country, and there are a variety of dishes that are served. However, some dishes are more common than others, such as samosas, pakoras, kebabs, and biryani. In some parts of the world, the meal may include soup, lentils, and bread. In some countries, fruits and juices are also an essential part of the iftar meal.

Apart from the food, iftar is also a time of giving and charity. Many Muslims choose to donate food, clothes, and money to the poor and needy during Ramadan. This practice is known as 'zakat,' which is one of the five pillars of Islam. It is believed that giving during Ramadan earns a higher reward from Allah.

In addition to the spiritual aspect, iftar also has health benefits. When Muslims fast during the day, they give their digestive system a much-needed break. The iftar meal is an opportunity to replenish the body with vital nutrients and energy.

In conclusion, iftar is an essential aspect of Ramadan for Muslims around the world. It is a time to break the fast, socialize with family and friends, reflect on one's spirituality, and give back to the community. It is also an opportunity to enjoy a variety of delicious and healthy foods. Overall, iftar is a time of celebration and gratitude, which strengthens the bond between Muslims and their faith.

.....

Correct Timing Of Iftar

1.Many of us eat iftar less than 1 minute later than the iftar schedule as a precaution. It's not right. It is forbidden to break iftar late. Again, in many places, iftar schedule is increased by 2 minutes to make the schedule. We should stay away from all this. Let's have a look at some authentic hadiths about fasting iftar.

✳ Narrated Sahl bin Sa`d: Allah's Messenger (ﷺ) said, "The people will remain on the right path as long as they hasten the breaking of the fast."(Sahih al-Bukhari-1957)

✳ Narrated Ibn Abi `Aufa: I was with the Prophet (ﷺ) on a journey, and he observed the fast till evening. The Prophet (ﷺ) said to a man, "Get down and mix Sawiq with water for me." He replied, "Will you wait till it is evening?" The Prophet said, "Get down and mix Sawiq with water for me; when you see night falling from this side, the fasting person should break his fast." (Sahih al-Bukhari-1958)

✳ Chapter: The Superiority of Hastening to Break the Fast, and the supplication to say upon Breaking it

Sahl bin Sa'd (May Allah be pleased with him) reported:
The Messenger of Allah (ﷺ) said, "People will continue to adhere to good as long as they hasten to break the Saum (fasting)."

[Al-Bukhari and Muslim].

Commentary: "Adhere to good" here means welfare of the religion as well as that of this world. Breaking the Saum early does not mean that it is terminated before the prescribed time. What it really means is without any delay after the sunset. One should not delay it for the mere reason that the rigour one has gone through in the Saum should be enhanced further, as is done by some Sufi. There is no merit in such things because the real merit lies in following the Sunnah of the Prophet (PBUH). Welfare of the Muslims will, therefore, come in the share of the Muslims because of their following the Prophet's Sunnah of breaking the Saum in the early moments of the prescribed time.(Riyadus Salihin-1241)
4.Abu Atiyyah said:
"Masruq and I entered upon Aishah and we said: 'O Mother of the Believers! There are two men from the Companions of Muhammad, one of them hastens to break the fasts and he hastens to perform Salat. The other delays breaking the fast and he delays the Salat.' She said: 'Which of them hastens to break the fast and hastens to perform the Salat?' We said that it

was Abdullah bin Mas'ud. She said: 'This is how the Messenger of Allah did it.' And the other was Abu Musa."Sunan at-Tirmidhi (Islamic foundation)-700)

Iftar schedule is published in our country - which add 1 minute or 2 minutes or 5 minutes to sunset time and write iftar time. But if you want to get the benefit mentioned in the hadith, you have to break the fast immediately after knowing the time of sunset.

2. Where do we get the correct time now? Finding the correct time is very easy in today's age. We always have internet with us now.You just surch google Sunset in .... After that you have to write the name of your area.As you think, I live in Barpeta. Then write :- Sunset in Barpeta.

....

Sunnah of Eid (Eidul Fitr)

> "Eid greetings can be exchanged by saying '"Taqabbalallahu minna wa minka'"

> Going to Masjid by eating dates or sweets.

> Fajr prayer with congregation.

> take a bath (Sunan Bayhaqi: 5920)

> Wear clean clothes.

> Use perfume.

> Eating dates on the day of Eid-ul-Fitr and appearing in the Idgah Maidan.(Sunan Ibn Majah-1754, Sahih Bukhari-953).

> Attending the Eidgah Maidan on foot.(Sunan Ibn Majah-1296.)

> Do not go back by the road you used to go to the Eidgah Maidan, return home by another route. (Sunan Ibn Majah-1299)

.....

Some of The Favorite Foods of Prophet(ﷺ)

According to Allah's command, whoever can implement the ideals of the Prophet (PBUH) in his life will be successful in this world and the hereafter.So some of the foods that Hazrat Muhammad (PBUH) liked to eat are mentioned here. Inshallah, these foods will definitely be in our favorite food list.

- **Goat Bones Mutton**. (Sunan Abu Dawud, Hadith No. 3780)

- **gourd:**
Narrated Anas bin Malik:
A tailor invited Allah's Messenger (ﷺ) to a meal which he had prepared. I went along with Allah's Messenger (ﷺ) and saw him seeking to eat the pieces of gourd from the various sides of the dish. Since that day I have liked to eat gourd. `Umar bin Abi Salama said: The Prophet, said to me, "Eat with your right hand."
(SahihBukhari,IslamiFoundationnumber:4987)
(Sahih Bukhari, International number: 5379)

- **cheese:**
Narrated Abdullah ibn Umar:
The Prophet (ﷺ) was brought a piece of cheese in Tabuk. He called for a knife, mentioned Allah's

name and cut it.(Sunan Abu Dawud (Islamic Foundation)Hadith No. 3776)

- **Vinegar:**

Jabir b. 'Abdullah reported that Allah's Apostle (ﷺ) asked his family for condiment. They (the members of his household) said:We have nothing with us but vinegar. He asked for it, he began to eat it, and then said: Vinegar is a good condiment, vinegar is a good condiment.(Sahih Muslim (Islamic Foundation)Hadith No. 5179)

- **Watermelon and fresh dates:**

Narrated Aisha, Ummul Mu'minin:
The Messenger of Allah (ﷺ) used to eat melon with fresh dates, and he used to say: The heat of the one is broken by the coolness of the other, and the coolness of the one by the heat of the other.(Sunan Abu Dawud (Islamic Foundation)Hadith No. 3793)

- **fresh dates and cucumbers:**

Narrated `Abdullah bin Ja`far:
I saw the Prophet (ﷺ) eating fresh dates with snake cucumbers.(Sahih Bukhari (Islamic Foundation)Hadith No. 5053)

- **butter:**

Narrated Abdullah ibn Busr ibn Atiyyah ibn Busr:
The Messenger of Allah (ﷺ) came to visit us and we offered him butter and dates, for he liked butter

and dates.(Sunan Abu Dawud (Islamic Foundation)Hadith No. 3794)

- **sweet and honey:**

Narrated `Aisha:

The Prophet (ﷺ) used to like sweet edible things and honey.(Sahih Bukhari (Tawheed Publication)Hadith No. 5682)

- **milk:**

Narrated Abu Huraira:

Allah's Messenger (ﷺ) said, "On the night of my Ascension to Heaven, I saw (the prophet) Moses who was a thin person with lank hair, looking like one of the men of the tribe of Shanua; and I saw Jesus who was of average height with red face as if he had just come out of a bathroom. And I resemble prophet Abraham more than any of his offspring does. Then I was given two cups, one containing milk and the other wine. Gabriel said, 'Drink whichever you like.' I took the milk and drank it. Gabriel said, 'You have accepted what is natural, (True Religion i.e. Islam) and if you had taken the wine, your followers would have gone astray.' "(Sahih Bukhari (Islamic Foundation)Hadith No. 3156)

- **dates:**

'A'ishah reported the Prophet(ﷺ) as saying:

A family which has no dates will be hungry.(Sunan Abu Dawud (Islamic Foundation)Hadith No. 3788)

- **olive.**(Riyadus Salehin, Hadith No. 1275)

....

Salah

Salah is one of the most important and fundamental pillars of Islam. It is the second pillar of Islam and is an essential part of a Muslim's daily life. The importance of prayer in Islam can be understood in the following ways:

1.Connection with Allah: Prayer is a way of establishing a direct connection with Allah, the Almighty. It is a means of communicating with Him, seeking His guidance and forgiveness, and expressing gratitude for His blessings.

2.Reminder of the purpose of life: Prayer reminds Muslims of the purpose of their existence, which is to worship Allah and follow His commands. It helps them to focus on their spiritual well-being and to maintain a close relationship with their Creator.

3.Purification of the soul: Prayer is a way of purifying the soul and seeking forgiveness for sins. It helps Muslims to rid themselves of negative thoughts and emotions and to maintain a state of inner peace and tranquility.

4.Community building: Prayer is not just an individual act of worship, but it is also a communal one. It brings Muslims together in the mosque to pray in congregation, strengthening their sense of community and brotherhood.

5.Discipline and self-control: Prayer requires Muslims to observe strict timings and perform specific actions, such as standing, bowing, and prostrating. This helps to develop discipline and self-control, which are essential qualities for a Muslim's personal and spiritual growth.

6.Protection from evil: Prayer is a means of seeking protection from evil and harm. It is a shield against the temptations of Satan and the trials and tribulations of this world.

In summary, prayer is a vital aspect of a Muslim's life, providing a means of connecting with Allah, purifying the soul, and maintaining a sense of community and discipline. Its importance cannot be overstated, and Muslims strive to perform their daily prayers with sincerity and devotion

....

What is the purpose of our life?

What is the purpose of our life?What is the purpose of our existence in this world?What do you think?Who can answer this question correctly?Can scientists answer this question? The answer is no;Philosophers are also unable to answer this question.

Our Creator, Almighty Allah Subhanahu wa Ta'ala can best answer this question.No one can give a better answer than him.

Allah did not create man without any purpose. Surely human creation has a purpose. Allah subhanahu wa ta'ala says about the purpose of human creation:

AND I DID NOT CREATE THE JINN AND MANKIND EXCEPT TO WORSHIP ME.(ADH-DHAARIYAT: AYAH NO. 56)

So it appears that man cannot lead his life aimlessly.

Then the purpose of our life is to worship allah.

....

Ramadan Quotes

- "The month of Ramadan is the world's most widespread fast and yet its teachings are minimally understood and practiced."

- "Fasting is, first and foremost, an exercise for identifying and managing adversity in all its forms. With faith, in full conscience, fasting calls women and men to an extra degree of self-awareness." - Tariq Ramadan

- "The philosophy of fasting calls upon us to know ourselves, to master ourselves, and to discipline ourselves the better to free ourselves. To fast is to identify our dependencies, and free ourselves from them." - Tariq Ramadan

- "The Prophet (PBUH) said, 'Whoever fasts in Ramadan with faith and seeking his reward from Allah will have his past sins forgiven.'" - Sahih Bukhari

- Ramadan is one of the doors of mercy flung wide open as an opportunity for soul cleansing.' — Ahmed Rehab.

- 'Sometimes you don't realize how special something is until you lose it. That's how I feel about Ramadan every year.' — Omar Suleiman.

◈ 'There's a battle going on inside you in Ramadan, and for 30 days Allah gives you the power to win.' — Nouman Ali Khan.

◈ 'Ramadan is a celebration of a faith known for great diversity and racial equality.' — Barack Obama.

◈ 'In Ramadan, you should eat less and think more.' — Tariq Ramadan

....

Ramadan in Quran

1.O you who have believed, decreed upon you is fasting as it was decreed upon those before you that you may become righteous -

Al-Baqara: Ayah No. 183

2.[Fasting for] a limited number of days. So whoever among you is ill or on a journey [during them] - then an equal number of days [are to be made up]. And upon those who are able [to fast, but with hardship] - a ransom [as substitute] of feeding a poor person [each day]. And whoever volunteers excess - it is better for him. But to fast is best for you, if you only knew.

Al-Baqara: Ayah No. 184

3.The month of Ramadhan [is that] in which was revealed the Qur'an, a guidance for the people and clear proofs of guidance and criterion. So whoever sights [the new moon of] the month, let him fast it; and whoever is ill or on a journey - then an equal number of other days. Allah intends for you ease and does not intend for you hardship and [wants] for you to complete the period and to glorify Allah for that [to] which He has guided you; and perhaps you will be grateful.

Al-Baqara: Ayah No. 185

4.It has been made permissible for you the night preceding fasting to go to your wives [for sexual relations]. They are clothing for you and you are clothing for them. Allah knows that you used to deceive yourselves, so He accepted your repentance and forgave you. So now, have relations with them and seek that which Allah has decreed for you. And eat and drink until the white thread of dawn becomes distinct to you from the black thread [of night]. Then complete the fast until the sunset. And do not have relations with them as long as you are staying for worship in the mosques. These are the limits [set by] Allah, so do not approach them. Thus does Allah make clear His ordinances to the people that they may become righteous.

Al-Baqara: Ayah No. 187

5.Indeed, We sent it down during a blessed night. Indeed, We were to warn [mankind].

Ad-Dukhaan: Ayah No. 3

....

THE GATE OF RAIYAN

Narrated Abu Huraira:
I heard Allah's Messenger (ﷺ) saying, "Anybody who spends a pair of something in Allah's Cause will be called from all the gates of Paradise, "O Allah's slave! This is good.' He who is amongst those who pray will be called from the gate of the prayer (in Paradise) and he who is from the people of Jihad will be called from the gate of Jihad, and he who is from those' who give in charity (i.e. Zakat) will be called from the gate of charity, and he who is amongst those who observe fast will be called from the gate of fasting, the gate of Raiyan." Abu Bakr said, "He who is called from all those gates will need nothing," He added, "Will anyone be called from all those gates, O Allah's Messenger (ﷺ)?" He said, "Yes, and I hope you will be among those, O Abu Bakr."(Sahihal-Bukhari **(Islamic** foundation)-3404)

GATES OF MERCY ARE OPENED

Abu Huraira reported Allah's Messenger (ﷺ) as saying:
When there comes the month of Ramadan, the gates of mercy are opened, and the gates of Hell are locked and the devils are chained, ."(Sahihal-Bukhari **(Islamic** foundation)-2366)

CHILDREN'S RAMADAN

Narrated Ar-Rubi'   bint   Mu'awadh:

"The Prophet (ﷺ) sent a messenger to the village of the Ansar in the morning of the day of 'Ashura' (10th of Muharram) to announce: 'Whoever has eaten something should not eat but complete the fast, and whoever is observing the fast should complete it.' "She further said, "Since then we used to fast on that day regularly and also make our boys fast. We used to make toys of wool for the boys and if anyone of them cried for, he was given those toys till it was the time of the breaking of the fast." (Sahihal-Bukhari (Islamic foundation)-1836)

FASTING THROUGHOUT THE YEAR

Narrated `Abdullah bin `Amr:
Allah's Messenger (ﷺ) was informed that I had taken an oath to fast daily and to pray (every night) all the night throughout my life (so Allah's Messenger (ﷺ) came to me and asked whether it was correct): I replied, "Let my parents be sacrificed for you! I said so." The Prophet (ﷺ) said, "You can not do that. So, fast for few days and give it up for few days, offer Salat (prayer) and sleep. Fast three days a

month as the reward of good deeds is multiplied ten times and that will be equal to one year of fasting." The Prophet (ﷺ) said to me, "Fast one day and give up fasting for two days." I replied, "I can do better than that." The Prophet (ﷺ) said to me, "Fast one day and give up fasting for a day and that is the fasting of Prophet David and that is the best fasting." I said, "I have the power to fast better (more) than that." The Prophet (ﷺ) said, "There is no better fasting than that." (Sahihal-Bukhari (Islamic foundation)-1852)

SMELL COMING OUT FROM THE MOUTH OF A FASTING PERSON IS BETTER IN THE SIGHT OF ALLAH THAN THE SMELL OF MUSK.

Narrated   Abu   Huraira:
Allah's Messenger (ﷺ) said, "Fasting is a shield (or a screen or a shelter). So, the person observing fasting should avoid sexual relation with his wife and should not behave foolishly and impudently, and if somebody fights with him or abuses him, he should tell him twice, 'I am fasting." The Prophet (ﷺ) added, "By Him in Whose Hands my soul is, the smell coming out from the mouth of a fasting person is better in the sight of Allah than the smell of musk. (Allah says about the fasting person), 'He has left his

food, drink and desires for My sake. The fast is for Me. So I will reward (the fasting person) for it and the reward of good deeds is multiplied ten times." (Sahihal-Bukhari (Islamic foundation)-1773)

THE FAST IS FOR ME

Narrated Abu Huraira:
Allah's Messenger (ﷺ) said, "Fasting is a shield (or a screen or a shelter). So, the person observing fasting should avoid sexual relation with his wife and should not behave foolishly and impudently, and if somebody fights with him or abuses him, he should tell him twice, 'I am fasting." The Prophet (ﷺ) added, "By Him in Whose Hands my soul is, the smell coming out from the mouth of a fasting person is better in the sight of Allah than the smell of musk. (Allah says about the fasting person), 'He has left his food, drink and desires for My sake. The fast is for Me. So I will reward (the fasting person) for it and the reward of good deeds is multiplied ten times." (Sahihal-Bukhari (Islamic foundation)-1773)

SEEING THE MOON

Narrated Ibn` Umar:
I heard Allah's Messenger (ﷺ) saying, "When you see the crescent (of the month of Ramadan), start fasting, and when you see the crescent (of the month of Shawwal), stop fasting; and if the sky is overcast (and you can't see it) then regard the month of Ramadan as of 30 days." (Sahihal-Bukhari (Islamic foundation)-1779)

IF SOMEBODY SHOULD FIGHT OR QUARREL WITH HIM, HE SHOULD SAY, 'I AM FASTING.

Narrated Abu Huraira:
Allah's Messenger (ﷺ) said, "Allah said, 'All the deeds of Adam's sons (people) are for them, except fasting which is for Me, and I will give the reward for it.' Fasting is a shield or protection from the fire and from committing sins. If one of you is fasting, he should avoid sexual relation with his wife and quarreling, and if somebody should fight or quarrel with him, he should say, 'I am fasting.' By Him in Whose Hands my soul is' The unpleasant smell coming out from the mouth of a fasting person is better in the sight of Allah than the smell of musk.

There are two pleasures for the fasting person, one at the time of breaking his fast, and the other at the time when he will meet his Lord; then he will be pleased because of his fasting." (Sahihal-Bukhari (Islamic foundation)-1783)

NONE OF YOU SHOULD FAST A DAY OR TWO BEFORE THE MONTH OF RAMADAN

Narrate Abu Huraira:
The Prophet (ﷺ) said, "None of you should fast a day or two before the month of Ramadan unless he has the habit of fasting (Nawafil) (and if his fasting coincides with that day) then he can fast that day." (Sahihal-Bukhari (Islamic foundation)-1793)

I WILL NEITHER PERFORM ANY NAWAFIL NOR WILL I DECREASE

Narrated Talha bin 'Ubaidullah:
A bedouin with unkempt hair came to Allah's Messenger (ﷺ) and said, "O Allah's Messenger (ﷺ)! Inform me what Allah has made compulsory for me as regards the prayers." He replied: "You have to offer perfectly the five compulsory prayers in a day and night (24

hours), unless you want to pray Nawafil." The bedouin further asked, "Inform me what Allah has made compulsory for me as regards fasting." He replied, "You have to fast during the whole month of Ramadan, unless you want to fast more as Nawafil." The bedouin further asked, "Tell me how much Zakat Allah has enjoined on me." Thus, Allah's Messenger (ﷺ) informed him about all the rules (i.e. fundamentals) of Islam. The bedouin then said, "By Him Who has honored you, I will neither perform any Nawafil nor will I decrease what Allah has enjoined on me. Allah's Messenger (ﷺ) said, "If he is saying the truth, he will succeed (or he will be granted Paradise).(Sahihal-
Bukhari (Islamic foundation)-1770)

THE PROPHET (ﷺ) USED TO KISS AND EMBRACE (HIS WIVES) WHILE HE WAS FASTING

Narrated`Aisha:
The Prophet (ﷺ) used to kiss and embrace (his wives) while he was fasting, and he had more power to control his desires than any of you. Said Jabir, "The person who gets discharge after casting a look (on his wife) should complete his fast."(Sahihal-Bukhari (Islamic foundation)-1804)

LYING

Narrated Abu Huraira:
The Prophet (ﷺ) said, "Whoever does not give up forged speech and evil actions, Allah is not in need of his leaving his food and drink (i.e. Allah will not accept his fasting.)" (Sahihal-Bukhari (Islamic foundation)-1782)

EAT AND DRINK UNTIL THE WHITE THREAD OF DAWN APPEARS TO YOU DISTINCT FROM THE BLACK THREAD (OF THE NIGHT)." (2.187)

Narrated Al-Bara:
It was the custom among the companions of Muhammad that if any of them was fasting and the food was presented (for breaking his fast), but he slept before eating, he would not eat that night and the following day till sunset. Qais bin Sirma-al-Ansari was fasting and came to his wife at the time of Iftar (breaking one's fast) and asked her whether she had anything to eat. She replied, "No, but I would go and bring some for you." He used to do hard work during the day, so he was overwhelmed by sleep and slept. When his wife came and saw him, she said, "Disappointment for you." When it was midday

on the following day, he fainted and the Prophet (ﷺ) was informed about the whole matter and the following verses were revealed: "You are permitted To go to your wives (for sexual relation) At the night of fasting." So, they were overjoyed by it. And then Allah also revealed: "And eat and drink Until the white thread Of dawn appears to you Distinct from the black thread (of the night)." (2.187) (Sahihal-Bukhari (Islamic foundation)-1798)

EAT SAHARI QUICKLY

Narrated Sahl bin Sa`d:
I used to take my Suhur meals with my family and then hurry up for presenting myself for the (Fajr) prayer with Allah's Messenger (ﷺ). (Sahihal-Bukhari (Islamic foundation)-1798)

WOMAN DOES NOT PRAY AND DOES NOT FAST ON MENSTRUATING

Narrated Abu Sa`id:
The Prophet (ﷺ) said, "Isn't it true that a woman does not pray and does not fast on menstruating? And that is the defect (a loss) in

her   religion."(Sahihal-
Bukhari (Islamic foundation)-1827)

DAY OF `ARAFAT

Narrated   Um   Al-Fadl   bint   Al-Harith:
"While the people were with me on the day of
`Arafat they differed as to whether the Prophet
(ﷺ) was fasting or not; some said that he was
fasting while others said that he was not fasting.
So, I sent to him a bowl full of milk while he was
riding over his camel and he drank it." (Sahihal-
Bukhari (Islamic foundation)-1865)

NO FASTING IS PERMISSIBLE ON THE TWO DAYS OF ID-UL-FITR AND `ID-UL-ADHA

Narrated   Abu   Sa`id Al-Khudri:
(who   fought   in   twelve   Ghazawat   in   the
company of the Prophet). I heard four things
from the Prophet (ﷺ) and they won my
admiration. He said; -1. "No lady should travel
on a journey of two days except with her
husband or a Dhi-Mahram; -2. "No fasting is

permissible on the two days of Id-ul-Fitr and `Id-ul-Adha; -3. "No prayer (may be offered) after the morning compulsory prayer until the sun rises; and no prayer after the `Asr prayer till the sun sets; -4. "One should travel only for visiting three Masjid (Mosques): Masjid-al-Haram (Mecca), Masjid-al- Aqsa (Jerusalem), and this (my) Mosque (at Medina). (Sahihal-Bukhari (Islamic foundation)-1871)

FAST ON THE DAY OF 'ASHURA'

Narrated   `Aisha:
Allah's Messenger (ﷺ) ordered (the Muslims) to fast on the day of 'Ashura', and when fasting in the month of Ramadan was prescribed, it became optional for one to fast on that day ('Ashura')   or   not.   (Sahihal-
Bukhari (Islamic foundation)-1875)

DONATIONS IN RAMADAN

Narrated   Ibn`   Abbas:
The Prophet (ﷺ) was the most generous amongst the people, and he used to be more so in the month of Ramadan when Gabriel visited him, and Gabriel used to meet him on every night of Ramadan till the end of the month. The Prophet (ﷺ) used to recite the

Holy Qur'an to Gabriel, and when Gabriel met him, he used to be more generous than a fast wind (which causes rain and welfare). (Sahihal-Bukhari (Islamic foundation)-1875)

THERE IS A BLESSING IN SEHRI

Anas (Allah be pleased with him) reported Allah's Messenger (ﷺ) as saying:
Take meal a little before dawn, for there is a blessing in taking meal at that time. (Sahihal-Bukhari (Islamic foundation)-2420)

IT IS PERMISSIBLE FOR A PERSON WHO HAS NOT FASTED FOR RAMADAN DUE TO PROBLEM SUCH AS DISEASE, TRAVEL AND MENSTRUAL SEASON, ETC., THEN IT IS PERMISSIBLE FOR HIM TO PERFORM THE FAST OF RAMADAN LATE UNTIL THE NEXT RAMADAN ARRIVES.

Salama reported:
I heard 'A'isha (Allah be pleased with her) as saying: I had to complete some of the fasts of Ramadan, but I could not do it but during the month of Sha'ban due to my duties to the Messenger of Allah (ﷺ) or with the Messenger of Allah (ﷺ). (Sahihal-Bukhari (Islamic foundation)-2558)

FASTING ON BEHALF OF THE DECEASED

Ibn 'Abbas (Allah be pleased with both of them) reported:
A woman came to the Messenger of Allah (ﷺ) and said: My mother has died, and fasts of a month are due from her. Thereupon he said: Don't you see that if debt was due from her, would you not pay it? She said: Yes (I would pay on her behalf). Thereupon he said: The debt of Allah deserves its payment more than (the payment of anyone else). (Sahihal-Bukhari (Islamic foundation)-2564)

FASTING IS A SHIELD

Abu Huraira reported Allah's Messenger (ﷺ) as saying: Fasting is a shield. (Sahih Muslim (Islamic foundation)-2576)

THERE ARE TWO THINGS TO BE HAPPY FOR A PERSON WHO FASTS.

Abu Huraira (Allah be pleased with him) reported Allah's Messenger (ﷺ) as saying:
Every (good) deed of the son of Adam would be multiplied, a good deed receiving a tenfold to seven

hundredfold reward. Allah, the Exalted and Majestic, has said: With the exception of fasting, for it is done for Me and I will give a reward for it, for one abandons his passion and food for My sake. There are two occasions of joy for one who fasts, joy when he breaks it, and joy when he meets his Lord, and the breath (of an observer of fast) is sweeter to Allah than the fragrance of musk. (Sahih Muslim (Islamic foundation)-2578)

HIS FACE FARTHER FROM THE FIRE (OF HELL) TO THE EXTENT OF SEVENTY YEARS' DISTANCE

Abu Sa'id al Khudri (Allah be pleased with him) reported Allah's Messenger (ﷺ) as saying:
Every servant of Allah who observes fast for a day in the way of Allah, Allah would remove, because of this day, his face farther from the Fire (of Hell) to the extent of seventy years' distance. (Sahih Muslim (Islamic foundation)-2582)

IF ANYONE FORGETS THAT HE IS FASTING AND EATS OR DRINKS

Abu Huraira reported Allah's Messenger (ﷺ) as saying:

If anyone forgets that he is fasting and eats or drinks he should complete his fast, for it is only Allah Who has fed him and given him drink. (<u>Sahih Muslim (Islamic foundation)</u>-2587)

THREE DAYS PER MONTH, THE DAY OF ARAFAT, THE DAY OF ASHURA, THE DAY OF MONDAY AND THURSDAY

Abu Qatada reported that a person came to the Messenger of Allah (ﷺ) and said: How do you fast? The Messenger of Allah (ﷺ) felt annoyed. When 'Umar (Allah be pleased with him) noticed his annoyance, he said: We are well pleased with Allah as our Lord, with Islam as our code of life, and with Muhammad as our Prophet. We seek refuge with Allah from the anger of Allah and that of His Messenger. 'Umar kept on repeating these words till his (the Prophet's) anger calmed down. Then Umar said: Messenger of Allah, what is the position of one who fasts perpetually? He (ﷺ) said: He neither fasted nor broke it, or he said: He did not fast and he did not break it. 'Umar said: What about him who fasts for two days and does not fast one day? He (ﷺ) said: Is anyone capable of doing that?

He ('Umar) said: What is the position of him who fasts for a day and doesn't fast on the other day? Thereupon he (the Holy Prophet) said: That is the fast of Dawud (peace be upon him). He ('Umar) said: What about him who fasts one day and doesn't fast for two days. Thereupon he (the Messenger of Allah) said: I wish I were given the strength to do that. Thereafter he (ﷺ) said: Fasting three days every month and that of Ramadan every year is a perpetual fasting. I seek from Allah that fasting on the day of 'Arafa may atone for the sins of the preceding and the coming years, and I seek from Allah that fasting on the day of Ashura may atone for the sins of the preceding year. (**Sahih Muslim (Islamic foundation)**-2617)

THE MOST EXCELLENT FAST AFTER RAMADAN

Abu Haraira (Allah be pleased with him) reported Allah's Messenger (ﷺ) as saying:
The most excellent fast after Ramadan is God's month. al-Muharram, and the most excellent prayer after what is prescribed is prayer during the night. (**Sahih Muslim (Islamic foundation)**-2626)

LAILAT-UL-QADR

Ibn Umar (Allah be pleased with them) reported Allah's Messenger (ﷺ) as saying:
He who is anxious to seek it (Lailat-ul-Qadr) should seek it in the last ten (nights of Ramadan). (<u>Sahih Muslim (Islamic foundation)</u>-2637)

Abu Sa'id al-Khudri (Allah be pleased with him) reported that Allah's Messenger (ﷺ) spent in devotion (in i'tikaf) the middle ten nights of the month of Ramadan, and when twenty nights were over and it was the twenty-first night, he went back to his residence and those who were along with him also returned (to their respective residences). He spent one month in devotion. Then he addressed the people on the night he came back (to his residence) and commanded them as Allah desired (him to command) and then said:
I used to devote myself (observe i'tikaf) during these ten (nights). Then I started devoting myself in the last ten (nights). And he who desires to observe i'tikaf along with me should spend the night) at his place of i'tikaf. And I saw this night (Lailat-ul-Qadr) but I forgot it (the exact night) ; so seek it;In the last ten nights on odd numbers. I saw (the glimpses of that dream) that I was prostrating in water and mud. Abu Sa'id al-Khudri said: It rained on the twenty-first night and the water dripped (from the roof) of the mosque at the place where the Messenger of Allah (ﷺ) observed prayer. I looked at him and as he completed the dawn prayer, (I found)

his face was wet with mud and water. (<u>Sahih Muslim (Islamic foundation)</u>)-2640)

NOTES